THE SCOTTISH TERRIER

THE SCOTTISH TERRIER

HOLLAND BUCKLEY

Foreword by Miriam Stamm

© 1998 William J. Davis's The Victorian Dog

Publisher Disclaimer: The content of this book, a re-print of a book written in the early twentieth century, is not intended for use as a modern-day dog breeding and dog care manual but rather as an entertaining, historical look at dog breeding and dog care of the past. The instructions and ideas are not necessarily meant for use today. Any literal usage is the sole responsibility of the reader.

Foreword copyright © Miriam Stamm, 1998

All rights reserved. No part of this publication may be reproduced, stored in a retrieval system or transmitted in any form by any means electronic, mechanical, photocopying or otherwise without first obtaining written permission of the copyright owner.

This edition published in 1998 by SMITHMARK Publishers, a division of U.S. Media Holdings, Inc., 115 West 18th Street, New York, NY 10011.

SMITHMARK books are available for bulk purchase for sales promotion or premium use. For details write or call the manager of special sales, SMITHMARK Publishers, 115 West 18th Street, New York, NY 10011; 212-519-1300.

ISBN: 0-7651-0812-7

Printed in China

10 9 8 7 6 5 4 3 2 1

Cover design: Hotfoot Studio

Library of Congress Cataloging-in-Publication Data

Buckley, Holland.
   The Scottish terrier / by Holland Buckley.
      p. cm.
   Originally published: London: Illustatrated Kennel News Co. Ltd., 1913.
    ISBN 0-7651-0812-7 (alk. paper)
    1. Scottish terrier.   I. Title.
SF429.S4B835 1998
636.755--dc21

98-3883
CIP

To E. Royston Mills, Esq., one of the most constant supporters and keen lovers of Scotland's National Terrier, and a faithful and unswerving friend to the writer, this work is dedicated.

FOREWORD

In the early 1900s, when Holland Buckley wrote this book, the Scottish Terrier was an uncommon sight outside of its native home, the Highlands of Scotland. The written history of the Scottish Terrier went back only about thirty years and much of it was spotty and inaccurate. This book was specifically intended as an introduction to successful breeding for the novice Scottie fancier, whom Buckley rightly saw as essential to the continued survival and development of the Scottish Terrier.

Buckley's book is not intended as a breed history—it mentions only briefly some of the great dogs of the early twentieth century and just a few of the influential breeders. The heart of this book is, instead, found in the chapters entitled "Breeding," "The Stud Dog," and "The Brood Bitch." In these sections Buckley eloquently spells out the basic principles of breeding good dogs, often with wit and gentle humor. Who can resist a writer who casually suggests, "The man or woman who breeds dogs in a haphazard way is a decadent who ought to be locked up." All breeders and Scottie enthusiasts, no matter how knowledgeable or experienced, can benefit from and enjoy this "bible" of the Scottish Terrier.

Miriam Stamm, 1998

Photo.] *[T. Fall, Baker Street.*
MR. HOLLAND BUCKLEY.

PREFACE.

THE matter contained in these pages has been written chiefly with the object of providing sign posts, as it were, for the novice owner and breeder, who, after all, is the mainstay of the breed.

To the "old parliamentary hand" small details are often vexing to the spirit that has soared far beyond first causes, but that they are of the most vital consequence to the breeder who has not "arrived" is an axiom which is proved many days in the year by those for whose guidance this book has chiefly been written—may I hope not in vain.

HOLLAND BUCKLEY.

CH. EMS CHEVALIER.

ORIGIN.

ORIGIN.

I DO not propose in this little work to go right back to the ark, or to claim such antiquity for the Scottish Terrier, who all the same is of undoubted " way back " origin. The claims for him are sometimes quaint, occasionally true, but often ridiculous.

That the three great breeds that are so popular to-day all descended from the Highland Terrier admits of no possible doubt. The Scottish Terrier, the West Highlander White, and the Skye, possess very many features and traits, which presumably prove their common origin.

Breeders have during the last twenty years considerably altered the conformation of the descendants of the original sires and dams, but I am inclined to the opinion that the breed type has been pretty generally adhered to. Unhappy indeed would be the breed's well wishers if the time ever came when the dour " auld farant " expression is eliminated from the *Tout ensemble* of the " chiel " from Scotland.

HISTORY.

CH. BAPTON WARRIOR.

CH. BAPTON NORMAN.

HISTORY.

A short *resume* of the modest "beginnings" of our now fashionable friend may not be uninteresting to that fast diminishing band of enthusiasts who possess a modicum of love for their companion, apart from mere monetary considerations. The records have it that their first time on earth, from a show point of view, was in 1877, when they were exhibited as Cairn Terriers. I have seen a picture in oil of a winner about this time, who rejoiced in the singularly euphonic name (to a Scotchman) of "Macgrath," and if the painting is a faithful portrait, this Terrier would be reckoned to-day a typical specimen. It is worth noting (and perhaps this may give pause to those foolish persons who declaim against the light brindle colour of some of our best modern specimens) that the aforesaid painting limns "Macgrath" as a light—a very light—red brindle.

Little must have been doing in the breed from 1877 until 1882, when the then Hon. Secretary of the Scottish Terrier Club, Mr. Ludlow, did some winning with a brace who in some ways are illustrious as forming the admitted " back blood " of the breed. The principal of these, " Splinter," is unquestionably the chief pillar of the Stud book, and he and " Bonaccord " were chiefly responsible for the production of Ch. " Rascal," to whom, through " Seafield," in my judgment, credit is due for the Scottish Terrier as we see him to-day. " Seafield " was the founder of the famous strain known by that prefix, and the only strain that could be relied upon for begetting high quality consistently even to this day. Certainly the most prepotent stud force in the history of the breed was his son " Seafield Rascal," who was the sire of Ch. " Heworth Rascal," a very nearly perfect dog, and also the best dog I ever judged of this breed, Ch. " Seafield Admiral." Ch. ' Bonaccord Sandy " sired our own Terrier " Master Sandy," who in turn was chiefly responsible for our three home-bred champions, Ch. " Clonmel Invader," Ch. " Clonmel Bride," and Ch. " Clonmel Dirk " (the latter a Canadian champion), and proved the immense prepotency of this line of blood.

It will be remembered that "Seafield Rascal" also sired Ch. "Bonaccord Peggy," a really beautiful specimen, as well as "Seafield Beauty."

Another celebrated son of "Seafield Rascal" was "Bonaccord Jock," bred by one of the most brainy breeders who ever entered any fancy. "Jock," like many a biggish terrier before him, proved his blood by begetting probably the most justly celebrated sire of modern times, "Laindon Lockhart," the possessor of the best eyes, bone and coat seen for years, and combined with immense terrier character Ch. "Laindon Locket" and Ch. "Clonmel Epic" gave splendid evidence of his great qualities. Another son of "Seafield," who proved the worth of his blood by siring infinitely better terriers than himself was "Camowen Laddie," who in double quick time got Ch. "Carter Laddie" and Ch. "Ems Chevalier," the latter an extraordinary dog, who at one show would be awarded v.h.c., and within a week would walk away with a Challenge Prize. Then there was Ch. "Bonaccord Nora," a truly remarkable bitch, who probably won more championships than any other half dozen bitches of the breed. And yet another wonderful terrier to prove my contention was Ch. " Ems Cosmetic," the greatest Scotch Terrier within my memory, and the nearest to come up to her owner's, Mr. W. L. McCandlish's brilliant description in the standard of the breed. It will come as no shock to those possessed of the privilege of Mr. McCandlish's acquaintance to know that his opinion is by no means in agreement with mine. Yet I fancy I am right, and am fortified with the reflection that a finer judge than either of us agrees with me, and she possesses the most ample opportunities of noting all " Cosmetic's " failings, which to my mind are worth quite a crowd of the virtues of many other front rank specimens.

The pedigrees of most of the strain dealt with can in the main be depended upon for accuracy. There have of course, been many other good terriers by other strains that have played their part, but in many cases their breeding is obscure. I personally have many grave doubts alike as to the correctness of pedigrees and also

FIVE CHAMPIONS.

CH. HUNTLEY DAISY.   CH. SEAFIELD BLOSSOM.   CH. CARTER LADDIE.   CH. BONACCORD NORA.   CH. BAYNING KISS.

of the wisdom of many deductions drawn from what were probably false premises put forward before the Kennel Club made faking by pedigrees impossible.

Ch. " Bonaccord Nora," now the property of Mr. J. Deane Willis, was one of the many fine terriers brought to London by Mr. W. M. Cummings. These numerous importations immensely popularized the breed in the South, for in a great measure they shifted the centre of the fancy due South.

About this time a great deal of dissension existed, which led to the formation of the South of England Scottish Terrier Club, with Mr. Royston Mills as its first President. The venture enlisted the whole-hearted support of the parent Club, and at once made a great hit. The Scottish Terrier ranks closed up solidly, and " true sport and the best dog to win " was the order of the day. An ill-advised attempt to boycott one of the finest and most independent judges that ever lived, at the Kennel Club's own Show, was repulsed with awful slaughter to the malcontents, and the final result was an entry which licked all records.

The astonishing success that Mrs. B. M. Hannay met with for a long period, proved the extraordinary force of the "Seafield" blood to which this genial lady clung with all the persistency of Icarus to his wheel.

Mr. Deane Willis also risked all his eggs in one basket, and the result has been the production of a number of terriers of the highest class, which culminated in the breeding of "Bapton Norman," who assuredly ranks with the best terriers of any time.

Yet again those genuine enthusiasts, the Misses Niven, have made history time and again by benching top notchers from Ch. "Marden Dobbin" in the days gone by and latterly "Marden Elfin," whose sire I and my partner, Mr. Mills, purchased, but we were minus the nous to keep him, and he is now an American Champion.

Instances could be multiplied, but the above prove absolutely that an adherence to well ascertained fact will lead the deserving breeder well in the way to breeding front rankers, while those whose preference lies with those who prate incessantly of the ultra value of the brilliant figures who have flashed now and again into the ring, but who have no blood that is of concrete service, will have had their beloved outcross, with the final and certain result of outcrossing themselves out of the Fancy.

Bapton Scottish Terriers.

"Bapton Blacksmith."   "Ch. Bapton Beryl."   "Ch. Bapton Dahlia."
FIRST PRIZE TEAM, KENNEL CLUB, 1912.
All sired by "Champion Bapton Norman."

BREEDING.

CH. MARDEN DOBIN

BREEDING.

If I were asked to name the greatest certainty in the breeding of Show stock of high class, I would at once select Scottish Terrier breeding, as being far, very far, in front of all other breeds of Terriers.

We may not get champions all the time, but the matrons, if of the true strain, and mated intelligently will get winners most of the time.

I have tried my hand at most other Terriers, so my experience is of some value ; and my experience is that of many others. For one thing there is not the rage to use winning dogs simply because they are winners, herein the valuable asset of level-headedness, the birthright of most Scotchmen, has worked splendidly for the breed.

The sires and dams by the greater proportion of the winning dogs for the last 15 years are or were quite unknown.

Here is a truth by no means hidden, and sufficient for those who run to read. The intense fascination that the breeding of blood stock exercises over the inhabitants of Great Britain is splendidly expressed in the care, intelligence, time and money lavished upon the breeding of the Scottish Terrier. Not for the enthusiasts of the breed the rule of thumb—by a Derby winner but of an Oaks heroine—but solid concentrated effort ; the nous to delve deeply into the pedigree of the sire and dam, and the avoidance of that terrible pitfall, head breeding—sans bone, coat, shape and character which more than in any other breed go to the making of the Scottish Terrier.

The most tragic confession of impotent effort I ever remember is the universal agreement amongst Fox Terrier breeders that with few exceptions " the big, oversized dog is the one that gets the winners." We certainly have found no such disability in the breed under notice, mainly because the correct size has been a *sine qua non* amongst nearly all judges, and the sizeable shed Scottish Terrier has not only handed down his weight but also the other points that go to make (when most other qualities are present) the " Die Hard," the most perfect Terrier on the Kennel Club list.

That this state of affairs may continue is the fervent wish of all the breed's supporters, for when it seems imperative in the history of any breed to go to giants for points that appear impossible for the right sized dog to transmit them. " The tune in us is lost, and whistling up back alleys to the moon will never find it."

I will presuppose that our budding fancier possesses a tight grip of his subject. He should be able to easily recognize the essential first aids to the ideal   Full well digested information will help him to shape to it in practice. The first thing that the beginner has to sit down and take notice of is the principle of heredity.

My own records amply prove that the puppies in the litter may favour the sire or dam to the entire exclusion of the grand parents. Occasionally some portion of the litter will throw back in type and colour to some quite distinct portion of their back blood, but the safest plan to follow is :—take it that the two parents together are responsible to the extent of one-half of every attribute inherited, one quarter being given to each parent. The four grand parents should be held responsible for one fourth, or separately, their share is one sixteenth each. The eight great-grandparents are vitally interested to the extent of one eighth.

The above is doubtless sufficiently rough and ready, and will also with experience show great variation. The urgent importance of a proper study of hereditary influence is provable on even a two generation experience.

My absolute conviction is, that the nearer the bitch approaches the standard the surer the results will be ; perhaps not so much from first attempts, but assuredly in those to follow.

The bitch's pedigree should of course show progeniture of quality and the correct type right through.

The clearest thinking and most astute breeder I ever met once wrote that a bitch should look feminine. I disagree entirely. The most strikingly successful results so far as I have seen have all or nearly all come from the masculine type of bitch, or one that

Mr. A. G. Cowley's Albourne Kennels,
HASSOCKS, SUSSEX.

AT STUD:

ALBOURNE SCORCHER.

Black Dog, Albourne Scorcher
- Devon Prince
  - West Point Duke
  - Albourne Nina
- Albourne Daisy
  - Ems Baritone
  - Ems Timely

Winner Championship Competitions, &c., &c. Undoubtedly one of the best little dogs ever bred, and sire of winners. Fee £2 2s.

ALBOURNE BOMBARDIER.

LITTLEBURY CHUM.

Littlebury Chum (Black)
- Ch. Ems Morning Nip
  - Ems Tonic
  - Ems Excuse
- Littlebury Mollie
  - Comowen Laddie
  - Glory O'Glen

A big winner Kennel Club, Taunton, Alexandra Palace, Southampton, Newbury, Redhill, Lewes, etc., etc. Sire of Winners. Fee £2 2s.

ALBOURNE AFTERTHOUGHT.

ALBOURNE BOMBARDIER.

Albourne Bombardier (Brindle)
- Abertay Bombardier
  - Ch Keppoch Dugald
  - Winnie
- Albourne Mistresses Double
  - Ch. Keppoch Dugald
  - Albourne Mistress

A big winner and essentially a Stud Dog. Fee 1 guinea.

ALBOURNE SCORCHER.

Winning dogs and bitches always for sale also puppies and dogs as companions.

ALBOURNE MODEL

is generally known as "Doggy." But this same gentleman in a singularly luminous and forceful fashion tells a truth which should sink doubly deep into the brains of every man or woman who aspires to winning the Challenge Cup at the great Joint Club Show :

"To breed dissimilar together in order to obtain the mean is a common method doomed from the outset to failure. The animal produced, even if the desired result is attained, is a detached unit without any ancestral backing. At best it can only be regarded as a new creation, without any finity of type, and it can be of breeding value only when mated with something similar to itself and very strongly descended from similar ancestors. It is, in fact, little removed from a mongrel."

Nothing can be more true, and tremendous regret will be avoided if this dictum is observed. For no breeder or breed will ever be of much account which lives on a parable of regrets. Mistakes which in the case of the master breeder are covered up and forgiven, are rarely forgiven to the novice breeder. For remember that what in the captain is but a choleric word, in the soldier is rank blasphemy.

The Shibboleth that "blood will tell," so dear to the heart, is true and only true when attention is directed to all essential and elemental characteristics by the whole ancestry, and thus immolation on the altar of fatuity is avoided.

For the more remote the tendency for evil the greater the force that will make itself felt for evil.

Prepotency is the most marvellous of all the forces, that at the same time helps and hinders. The term itself is of vague enough meaning, and proceeds from the power possessed by some dogs of stamping their stock with some outstanding characteristic, which is not traceable to immediate parents or along the line of near ancestry.

Prepotency is sometimes all for good, but in the main is a bar to quick progress. The "rule of thumb" mating has stocked three continents with well bred untypical terriers. Men who ought to know better (I am an instance in point) ofttimes send their bitches to a sire who happens to be champion at the moment. The breeder's object should be to combine desirable points and characteristics and to eliminate everything that is not typical or desirable. We might not be able to afford to buy a bitch excelling so in points that she could herself be a winner in good company, but we can at least insist that the blood of the future matron should be untainted by evil influences.

Consanguinity is yet another powerful force that in my opinion has not been used nearly as much as opportunity offers. All the strongest reproductive forces in both dog and bitch proceed from inbreeding. Type is fixed, or ought to be. Certain essentials are there for the asking, and dogs that are prepotent in the best sense are available to perpetuate high class animals. Winners are numerous, and the barometer of the breed tells unfailingly of big entries and winners from large and small kennels indiscriminately. Rational inbreeding is practised by the leading owners of all big kennels, and the novice, by careful study of methods, can easily reap the same successful results.

A long course of inbreeding would doubtless sap the constitution of any breed, however hardy. Weakly, puny pups, and barren bitches would be the heavy price to be paid for such lunacy. I simply advise rational inbreeding.

A GROUP OF MR. H. R. B. TWEED'S SCOTTISH TERRIERS.
Left to right :—1. Laindon Laddie (Laindon Lockhart ex Tosker's Sister). 2. L. Lockhart (Bonaccord Jock ex Ch. Bonaccord Nora.) 3. L. Lennox (Ch. Ems Chevalier ex Bonaccord Ivy). 4. L. Lovelace (L. Lockhart ex Tosker's Sister). 5. Ch. L. Leda (L. Laddie ex L. Polly). 6. L. Lottie (Ems Tonic ex Bonaccord Jewel). 7. L. Leslie (L. Lockhart ex L. Jean).

CH. CARTER LADDIE

CH. KEPPOCH DUGALD.

THE STUD DOG.

THE STUD DOG.

No time is ill spent that has for its object the founding of a line of pedigree stock, and the selection of the sire of your prospective litter is probably of vital consequence to your future. The man or woman who breeds dogs in a haphazard way is a decadent who ought to be locked up ; for it is this class of breeder who succeeds in overflowing our show benches with worthless rubbish. I am sorry to say that the most obvious truth to any prominent owner of a stud dog is that the greater number of novices decide upon the choice of a stud dog without thought, or the use of the most ordinary intelligence. They may probably have never seen their choice, but have disinterred him from the columns of the canine press. He is without a doubt described as the " best Scottie living " by the owner.

But my advice is to see the dog, make a careful study of his pedigree, talk the matter over with any of our most successful breeders (they are almost without an exception sportsmen), and *then* take your plunge. If possible accompany your bitch and see the service performed. The bitch will be all the easier for it, and the owner of the stud dog will invariably be glad to see you. Do not wait until your Scottish lady is due, but get busy and look for the possible mate in good time. Above all don't be tempted by a cheap fee. That which is cheap is proverbially nasty, and this is particularly true of stud dogs. And remember that a show record is not all the proof you want of a dog's worth. Some of the best dogs that I have known never possessed bench records.

Photo   Hedges, Lytham.
CH. HEWORTH BANTOCK.

Photo   T. Fall, Baker St., W.
LAINDON LOCKHART.

THE BROOD BITCH.

THE BROOD BITCH.

Let your bitch be fit, not fat. Most bitches when in use are shut up just as soon as the period of œstrum arrives, and rarely gets her proper exercise, a fatal mistake, as she requires double the work when in season. This will keep her blood right, and also keep her in the finest possible condition for certain breeding.

Always " worm " the brood bitch before mating, and use one of the well tried vermifuges on the market.

After the first month of gestation she should be given plenty of walking exercise on the roads. Maintain her full interests in all things, she will be the healthier for it.

See that meat, both raw and cooked, is given to her in plentiful quantities, with, especially towards the last two weeks, plenty of milk and brown bread. At least three days before the whelps are due give two tablespoonfuls of olive oil night and morning, and also rub the passage with the same bland oil.

Phosphate of lime can also be strongly recommended as a certain bone former.

A place that is quite free from visits from other dogs is very desirable, and the bitch should be used to her whelping home at least two weeks before she is due. After the long expected family have arrived, for at least three days, only slops should be given. After that, all things being in order, cooked meat and plenty of it should be given. Milk and Lactol, Malt Milk or Plasmon (all of which have given satisfactory results) will also be found of great service.

At three weeks the pups should be taught to lap. Some do so quite naturally, and those that are backward can easily be induced, especially if the milk be thickened with sugar. From the fourth week onwards meat scraped and minced, the former for choice, can be given, with soup thickened with one of the above mentioned milk foods. Big bones will also not only amuse the pups but assist their bone and coat generally.

The pups should be weaned at six weeks, the bitch being gradually removed. My own practice is to draft the pups out to walk at that age, but first they should be dosed for worms, at least twice.

Periodic visits should be made to the cottages where your future champion is maturing. He may not be thriving, and a tonic or a fresh home is often necessary. Do not forget to buy both collar and lead for your cottager, who will attend to that part of your pup's education which is greatly inducive to the acquirement of that gay and debonair carriage that makes the " Diehard " so popular. At eight months, if not before, the pup should be brought in. The coat will want attention, and the real training will begin to fit the puppy for the Show Ring. The best possible practice is lead work amongst your other terriers. A few pieces of hard-baked liver thrown for him to catch will invariably bring him from a position of slackness to one of extreme alertness.

Retrieving golf balls, too, is fine practice, and will always make the slackest shower into a smart, bright dog.

Never be hasty or unkind, should your pup annoy you by his inability to learn quickly. Don't forget that he is very sensitive, easily bullied, and cowed by harsh measures. Do not spare the brush and comb. Use all legitimate measures to show your dog to the best advantage. Practice him weeks before the show to jumping into the hamper that he will travel in. Show him that it is a privilege, he will then, when the fateful day arrives, feel less like a prisoner going to the scaffold.

Be quite prepared when the Judge takes the ring, or your puppy will be dragged in by a keeper, who has no soul for the business on hand.

It is the business of the Judge to find out the weak points of your exhibit : it is yours to do all possible not to let them be too apparent.

Don't purposely deceive, but use every legitimate means to present your dog to the best possible advantage. Your dog will look all the better if you do not practise the art of the barber on his ears. A little hair removed, and the ears sometimes look enormous.

Should you possess any thoughts of buying dogs from the Judge, refrain from writing him just before the Show, it won't improve your chance with the gentlemen who usually judge Scottish Terriers.

Remember that the breed has been brought to the present position by many sacrifices made by the founders of the Scottish Terrier Club, England, and by none more than its present skipper, Mr. W. L. McCandlish, who will, all things being level, see you through for membership, which consummation will be of inestimable advantage to you in the pursuit of your hobby. Use all your store of commonsense business acumen in your fancy in exactly the same ratio as you would in any other serious business undertaking, and your reward will not improbably be commensurate with your labours.

Madam Opportunity will surely knock at your door some day, when you will captivate the fancy by the exhibition of your special cuvee of champions.

STANDARD OF POINTS.

LADY EVA HEATHCOTE WITH CH. HINTON DORCAS.

STANDARD OF POINTS OF THE SCOTTISH TERRIER.

Skull — Proportionally long, and covered with short, hard hair. It should not be quite flat, as there should be a slight stop, or drop, between the eyes.

Muzzle — Very powerful, and gradually tapering towards the nose, which should always be black and of good size. The jaws should be level, having the front upper teeth level with, or just overlapping the under ones.

Eyes — Set wide apart, of a dark hazel colour; small, piercing, very bright, and rather sunken.

Ears — Small and erect. They should always be sharp pointed. The hair on them should not be long, but velvety, without any fringe at the top.

Neck — Short, thick, and muscular; strongly set on sloping shoulders.

Chest — Broad in comparison to the size of the dog, and proportionately deep.

Body	Short, but well ribbed up, and exceedingly strong in hindquarters.
Legs and Feet	Both fore and hind legs should be short, and very heavy in bone, the former being as straight as possible, and well set on under the body, as the Scottish Terrier should not be out at elbows. The hocks should be bent, and the thighs very muscular: the feet strong and thickly covered with short hair. The fore feet being larger than the hind ones, and well let down to the ground.
The Tail	Which is never cut, should be about 7 inches long; carried with a slight bend, and often gaily.
The Coat	Should be of two textures, the outer long and intensely hard and wiry, and the under short and soft and exceedingly dense.
Size	About 16 lbs. to 18 lbs. for a bitch, and 18 lbs. to 20 lbs. for a dog.
Colours	Steel or iron-grey, brindled or grizzled, black, sandy, and wheaten. White markings are objectionable, and can only be allowed on the chest, and that to a small extent.

General Appearance The face should wear a very sharp, bright, active expression, and the head should be carried up. The dog (owing to the shortness of his coat) should appear to be higher on the leg than he really is, but at the same time he should look compact, and possessed of great muscle in the hind quarters. In fact, a Scottish Terrier, though essentially a terrier, cannot be too powerfully put together. He should be from 9 inches to 12 inches in height.

FAULTS.

Muzzle Either under or over hung.
Eyes Large, light coloured, or round.
Ears Large, round at the point or drop.
Coat Any silkiness, wave, or tendency to curl is a serious blemish, as is also an open coat.
Size Any specimens over 20 lbs. should not be encouraged.

EMS MORNING NIP.

THE KENNEL—HOW ARRANGED.

THE KENNEL—HOW ARRANGED.

If the dog is kept simply for family companionship no kennel will be needed. It is absolute cruelty of the worst description to keep a lively, bright terrier chained up to a box. There is also solid reasons against the practice from a purely financial point of view, for your dog will deteriorate in shoulders and elbows from jumping continually at the limit his chain will go out. His disposition, also, will be ruined, and from a bright, active companion he will gradually degenerate into a morose cur.

Never chain a dog to a fence or rail. This is in the greatest degree dangerous, as the dog will probably jump over and choke himself.

Should you be only keeping one dog for a companion surely the house is his proper position, but if you must put him out, this method will be found the best:— a strong wire, 15 to 20 feet in length, with a solid metal ring sliding its whole length, to which attach the swivelled chain. This will give him ample exercise.

CARE OF PUPPIES.

ALBOURNE SLOGAN.

CARE OF PUPPIES.

I am personally dead in favour of drafting all pups out to cottage walkers as soon as they leave the dam. But when this, for various reasons, cannot be done, the greatest care must be exercised if the pups are to mature into healthy specimens. The best time to separate the whelps from the dam is at six weeks old, but it is distinctly advisable to "worm" them first, say, at five weeks, while on the dam, and then again at six weeks. The fæces of all puppies should be carefully scrutinized to ascertain if they are infested with parasitic worm life. Often a puppy will be full of worms without showing signs. The best plan is to give a dose of castor or olive oil, and then watch developments.

If you see signs of the long, curled, round worm, whose ends are pointed, usually accompanied by slimy stools, treat at once with areca nut for pups past six weeks old. The dose should be one grain to every pound the pup weighs, being especially careful to fast the puppy for quite twenty-four hours, and always follow up at an hour's interval with a dose of castor oil warmed up. The powdered areca nut is very bitter, so better results will be obtained if the doses are made up into capsule form. The presence of tape worm is readily detected by watching if the fæces have clinging to them little short segments, which are lively and active when dropped.

The head of the tape worm is a dark purple spot, and unless the dose is thorough enough to kill the worm, so that the head releases its hold upon the walls of the intestine the parasite grows again in an astonishingly short period. It will be seen from this the importance of watching for the head of the tape worm, so if the first dose is not effectual a second treatment will be found necessary after an interval of ten days. It is of great importance not to feed the subject for at least four hours after administration of the medicine, and then only with thickened soups. The digestive organs should not be overtaxed with much solid food.

Should your puppies be allowed to get thoroughly infested with these enemies to their life, their ailments will multiply fast, for it is impossible for a puppy in this state to thrive. The tissues of the intestines will become inflamed, and cause acute indigestion. The tongue will be coated white and the gums will be of an unhealthy pale colour. The eyes will run and after eating the puppy will look bloated and there will be a great attenuation of flesh. The coat will look rough and unkempt, with probably rickets and great weakness of the joints, all of which will be avoided if owners will only take time by the forelock and dose their young stock whenever the presence of worms is suspected, and they nearly always are present in young pups. The golden rule is to be always after them.

The weaning time really should always begin at one month, when a little Lactol should be given. The pups may be shy of lapping at first, but your finger smeared around their gums with either Lactol or the broth from boiled beef or mutton will soon awaken desire for closer aquaintance with the luxuries of canine life.

Always cool the food before putting it down. A shallow pan is best, but do no more than cover the bottom and replenish as it is cleared up.

I am personally not a strong believer in cow's milk, or biscuits or bread, but am all out for soups, boiled meats, bones, fats, Lactol with a pinch (to be increased later to a half-spoonful) of Phosto, the latter a wonderful preparation for bone forming.

Lactol is certainly the finest scientific discovery of the decade, for puppies simply love it and thrive in the most amazing manner upon it. The finest Airedale I ever bred was given little else for five months, and at five months his bone and size were equal to an eight months' puppy. The bone and substance of Ch. "Scotia Chief" was often remarked upon, as was that of "Clonmel Mark," all fine testimonials to this truly wonderful preparation. Three to four times a day should the above foods be given in such quantities as can readily be fixed upon by a discerning owner. The golden rule is to feed little and often. Never allow them to bloat; and invariably take the feeding troughs away if not cleared up. The habit of leaving food about to become stale has caused losses in many a promising litter. The pups should be watched carefully for the first few days to see if the change of diet is working properly. If there is any tendency to undue looseness of the bowels, or greyish fæces, give each a dose of castor oil, and follow with Lactol only for a time. But if they still show signs of intestinal disturbance, created by non-assimilation of food, give daily a pinch of flower of sulphur in their food, until their bowels act normally again.

Should, despite all your care, your puppy get into that condition known as rickets, all your care and attention must be lavished instantly upon the sufferer.

This disease is a general weakening of the muscles of the knee or pastern joint of the fore legs, causing the legs to be very weak at the joints; the knees turning in and feet well out or right down flat upon the pasterns. The fore arm goes weak and bows out, the bones eventually curving out. The causes are damp kennels and floors; malnutrition, the bones and muscles being insufficiently nourished; and—of course—worms. Add to the diet outlined a spoonful of calcium phosphate of lime. This should be sufficient for six puppies. Add to the diet twice daily raw meat, cut up fine. Give also small doses of cod liver oil daily; but always start the treatment by a vermifuge.

It is obviously the better plan to avoid the conditions that make for ricketty whelps than to have to bother with the cure of the pups when afflicted. A brood bitch infested with worms or one that has not had sufficient bone forming foods, will more often than not whelp litters prone to rickets and most other ailments.

EXERCISE.

EXERCISE.

Puppies exercise themselves in play if allowed sufficient room. Be careful not to give youngsters hard runs following bikes or horses : this method is a serious tax upon their systems. During the fourth month accustom your pup to collar and lead. This will be found a very simple matter if proper encouragement is given. It is half the battle in selling a dog, as it at once puts the pup on good terms with the new owner. Nothing is more calculated to annoy a probable purchaser than to receive a dog that hugs the rails or has to be carried or dragged along. Some will be quite obdurate and fierce during the first lessons. But a little petting to these and firmness and kindness with the timid, scared ones, and they will soon discover that they are not going to a funeral, and that it is far easier to follow than to hold back.

It is of the greatest importance to thoroughly instil confidence in a young puppy. Should he be unduly frightened by any untoward situation take him firmly in hand and try your best to show the utter needlessness of his brain storm. Too much confinement, it is to be remembered, is as bad as too much liberty.

BATHING AND GROOMING.

BATHING AND GROOMING.

Most people wash their dogs regularly. Unless preparing a puppy for a special purpose, do not bath him at all, at least not artificially, but use him to swimming in a pond or the river, never forgetting to give him a good gallop and a rub down afterwards.

By this system your puppy will be free from colds and kindred ailments. Use disinfectants and soaps in your kennels and in cleaning feeding vessels.

A few minutes spent each day with a comb and dandy brush will keep the coat in tip top condition, and the skin supple and healthy.

BONACCORD & LAINDON STRAINS.

Puppies always for sale. House-born and reared. A few dogs boarded as pets, not in kennels

MOOR COTTAGE,
  WATER END,
    HEMEL HEMSTEAD,
      HERTS.

PUPS FROM "BONACCORD BARBARA," by "Laindon Laddie."

PREPARING FOR SHOW.

PREPARING FOR SHOW.

Always start with plenty of time in hand. The very easiest Terrier of all to condition for show is the Scottish Terrier. Exercise and the best of feeding are essential Not too heavy in flesh, but well developed muscle and great hindquarters is the goal to aim at. Except for one good clean up never wash a Scottie. Most soaps will soften the hardest coat. The coat should be combed and brushed every day for quite a month before the Show. Constant attention to this will bring out all or most of the old coat, and bring out in bold relief the new. A few eggs, raw, will improve the " sheen " of the coat wonderfully, and Fuller's earth brushed in and out will tend to make the coat sparkle with condition.

SHOWING AND HANDLING.

SHOWING AND HANDLING.

It is clear that no pains taken to show a dog to the very best advantage when in the ring are thrown away. The best part of the battle is over by the classy terrier " putting it all in " when in front of the Judge.

Let your Terrier get it well into his head that when on the lead is the proper time to show his paces. He will then associate pleasure and action with the idea of being led, and when wanted to do so will eagerly respond and stand to attention. The more life a dog exhibits on the lead the better he will show in a ring full of dogs. A Judge has only a limited amount of time at his disposal, and is not empowered to give points to exhibits which are not obvious but which might be if better handled. A little scented liver or a ball are very useful. Always be keen to keep your Terrier's legs and feet in a typical and uniform condition. Your motto should be head and tail up all the time. Keep your charge always in full view of the Judge, who is there to compare him with the rest of the competitors.

You seriously prejudice your dog's chance by keeping him behind other dogs. You should never take your eyes off your Terrier until the awards are made, which we should all train ourselves to receive with stoic equanimity as being the matured and honest opinion of the Judge. Be a good winner and a good loser.

If the day goes against you, your selection of Shows and Judges is sufficiently large to try again. The awards are after all only the expression of one man's judgment, and the best of them at times overlook virtues as well as they sometimes miss bad faults, which if seen would materially have altered the prize list. No man is infallible, not even a Scotchman judging a "Diehard!" The opinion which you will receive at from three to four different Shows will soon settle the limitations and winning chance of your entry, and the owner's education will have advanced greatly in appreciation of his dark horse's type and quality.

CHAMPION "LAINDON LOCKET,"
by Laindon Lockhart ex Laindon Liza.

DISTEMPER.

Distemper

Distemper has mostly been regarded as a well nigh fatal disease to dogs, and when one thinks of the tremendous time that has elapsed since Aristotle (when the disease was first written about), small wonder at the universal dread with which the name is received. It was probably imported into Europe for the first time in the middle of the 18th century, from Peru. Spain appears to have been the country where the germs first found a domicile, after which it spread to France and Germany. It probably reached England about 1760.

In my own time distemper has been regarded as Plague, Nervous Febris Nucosa, Typhoid, and even Typhus. Old authors constantly have written of it as true Small Pox, the great authority, Trasbot, agreeing, a large number of unsuccessful experiments were made. But Dupuis demonstrated the falsity of this view by recent experiments, for in no case was he able to produce immunity against distemper by vaccinating young dogs.

Blain recognized at an early period that distemper was spread by an infective matter, and as a consequence numerous artificial transmission experiments were made with its virus. Trastowe proved that young dogs that had not suffered from the disease were susceptible to it, and that it could be both directly and indirectly transmitted. Dogs were inoculated from 30 days to four months old, by introducing nasal discharge mixed with the contents of the veticle, into small incisions in the abdominal walls. The usual period of incubation varied from seven to ten days. Infection was also produced by cohabitation, a thorough infection. Venuta proved that the contagion was fixed as well as volatile, and would still retain vitality and bear drying in the air up to a certain degree. Most of the authorities agree that the increase of the internal temperature is the first symptom, and also that one attack generally confers immunity, although this latter is by no means my experience. I have known many mild cases in which recovery takes place from five to ten days, but in prolonged cases I have had dogs down two months. The nasal discharge unquestionably loses most of its virulence in sixteen days, and it is also certain that the contents of the pustules are quite ineffective for the transmission of the disease. No writers agree now that distemper is not a contagious infective disease. No chemist has yet been able to obtain pure cultures, and their successful transmission. Although it is probably easier to transmit by cohabitation than by inoculation, it is probably taken from the air during inspiration. The great predisposing cause of the disease is chill, mostly brought on by open air exposure during cold, wet weather. Washing and bathing will facilitate the penetration of the virus by weakening the vital forces. I have never yet seen a cold by itself produce distemper, but a weakening of the respiratory mucous membranes will certainly predispose.

The mistaken fallacy that meat is injurious to dogs has probably made many thousands of victims, as bread and its concomitants undoubtedly weaken dogs, for whom meat is the only appropriate food. The practice of allowing bitches to bring up large litters is a fruitful cause of distemper, as one of the chief predisposing causes is weak unhealthy stock.

Although cold and wet are causes almost certain to bring on an attack of the disease, my own experience is that the great majority of the outbreaks occur in the summer, warmth greatly favouring the development of the contagion. I would like in plain language to describe the usual symptoms, which vary greatly, and are chiefly those of an infectious catarrh of the eyes, and the digestive and respiratory organs, which catarrhal symptoms frequently become complicated with disturbance of the brain, and in very many cases with pneumonia. The division into various forms may be shortly put under the headings of catarrhal, nervous, enanthematic distemper, or gastric distemper and pulmonary distemper. Mostly several organs are affected at the same time, but it does frequently occur that the pure form is only present, without any complication.

The first symptoms to look to are decreased vivacity, dainty appetite, trembling and shivering, warm and dry state of the nose, and intense emaciation, so that in some cases the dog will fall away to a mere skeleton in a few days. The nasal discharge will usually start within seven days from date of infection, but the eyes are usually the first to give warning, conjunctivitis being the primary symptom, but the rise in temperature will tell its own tale with unerring accuracy, the temperature rising in the most ominous manner from the time of incubation, and this should be treated when it rises to a great height, for by its persistent action it threatens the heart. Febrifuges antipyrine 2 to 5 grains and antifebrine 2 to 10 grains should be given. The temperature is very quickly reduced with these agents, and 2 grains every hour may be given until the temperature is nearly normal. The effect of quinine is, I think, not nearly so marked as the above.

Calomel is unquestionably a fine drug for the gastric form of distemper, but it acts with such power that it should rarely be used except under the advice of a veterinary surgeon. In an Airedale I have frequently had good results from the administration, twice a day, in doses of $\frac{1}{2}$ grain. Calomel is a fine disinfectant, but Salol is almost as good, and may be given instead three times a day in 2 grain doses. The bronchial form should be treated by severe disinfection of the mucous membrane respiratory portion by inhalations of Creolin.

An emetic is sometimes of great value in the commencement of the disease. A good one will be found in the following :— Hydroclorate of apomorphia $\frac{1}{10}$ grain in a teaspoonful of water. When given injected under the skin it acts almost instantaneously.

Or Tartar emetic, which is better, $\frac{1}{2}$ a grain shaken dry on the back of the tongue. If vomiting should not be induced in about 10 minutes, a few spoonfuls of warm water should be given.

Or Ipecacuanha wine a teaspoonful and a half, repeated in ten minutes, if vomiting not induced, and again ten minutes later if necessary.

In cases of emergency common salt may be given, sufficient to cover a shilling, in warm water.

Should there be diarrhœa a small dose of castor oil at the commencement of the attack is beneficial, but should the symptoms continue after the effects of the oil have passed off give 10 grains of Carbonate of bismuth three or four times a day before food.

Or the following mixture, Laudanum 1 drachm, Tincture of Rhubarb 4 drachms, Peppermint water to 4 ounces, two teaspoonfuls three times a day.

Or the following pills may be tried, Extract of kino 1 drachm, Powdered Ipecacuanha 12 grains, Powdered Opium 4 grains, divide into 12 pills, one to be given 3 or 4 times a day.

If the motions are very offensive give 4 grains of Salol 3 or 4 times a day also.

In Dysenteric Diarrhoea give at once a dose of Castor oil and laudanum, 2 teaspoonfuls of oil mixed with 5 drops of laudanum. About 6 hours afterwards commence to give Carbonate bismuth 10 grains every 3 or 4 hours, also 2 or 3 times a day give an enema of thick boiled starch, 2 teaspoonfuls mixed with 5 drops of laudanum. The enema should be just warm, given very slowly, and the dog should be kept quiet for a short time afterwards to prevent his ejecting it.

The following mixture may be tried if the symptoms continue in spite of the bismuth :— Chlorodyne 2 drachms, Prepared chalk 4 drachms, Tr. Catechu 4 drachms, Sol. Gum Acacia 1 ounce, Water to 6 ounces, two teaspoonfuls every 3 or 4 hours.

For cough give the following mixture, Liquor Morphia 2 drachms, Syrup of Squills 1 ounce, Syrup of Lemon 1 ounce, Water to 3 ounces, two teaspoonfuls 3 or 4 times a day.

When it is difficult to give a mixture the following pills may be tried, Hydroclorate of Morphia ½ grain, Powdered Ipecacuanha 2 grains, Powdered Rhubarb 5 grains, Compound Squill Pill 12 grains, mix and divide into 12 pills, one to be given night and morning. A dose of aperient medicine should occasionally be given if dog is constipated.

Pustules generally show themselves at the commencement of the disease, but it can be considered an excellent sign of the dog returning to normal conditions when breaking out of the skin occurs on the body and particularly under the thighs and stomach. Moist sore places may be dried by dusting Tanniform on the places. Glycerine should be applied to the crusts of the dried up sores, which will hasten removal.

Nursing is, of course, the handmaiden to complete recovery. Fresh air, warmth, comfort, absolute quiet, chills guarded against with the greatest care, and the strength kept up day and night, will mostly bring about healthy convalescence.